The Art Show Gypsy

The trials and tribulations of selling your art in street fairs.

By Judi Forney

Lady of the Wood Publishing

Email: forneyja@aol.com

Website: www.ladyofthewoodpublishing.com
Website: www.judiforneyart.com

Library of Congress,
United States of America

Certificate of Registration
TXu 1-867-039 May 8, 2013

Create Space
ISBN-13978-1493670611
ISBN 10 1493670611

Introduction

The old adage is, "Be careful what you wish for because it might come true," completely applies to my adventure into marketing my art. I made many discoveries about myself via my careening journey; the most important discovery I made was, don't send an accountant out to sell anything, sales ability is a missing piece of their personality. There were reasons why I hid out in an office for so many years "flying under the radar," I simply didn't want to be noticed but standing in front of a display of my art definitely focused attention on me, while I tried to compete in a field that was so far beyond my realm of experience.

Perhaps being exposed to the elements brought out the worst in me, who knows? I can remember making some pretty acerbic and fractious statements to people who wanted to talk about art with me. As memory serves me, my response to someone who had the temerity to ask, "I notice your painting has an old date on it, will that affect how long the painting will last?" I looked at her like she was a total idiot and said, "Have you ever visited a museum and looked at the oil paintings that are hundreds of years old?" She responded, "Yes", well I responded, "That answers your question." So much for schmoozing the customers and encourage them to buy my art.

I remain my own worst enemy when it comes to marketing my art. As far as I know, there are no personality enhancement pills that I could take that would change me from an accountant to a salesperson. My suggestion to other artists out there who decide to go on a marketing junket, is to hire someone who excels at sales and just stay at home continuing to create your art, that would be a true "win, win" scenario.

Dedication

This book is dedicated to my friends who have stood by me no matter how many crazy schemes I continue to come up with. Their love and support keeps me going on my meandering path through life. I thank them for adding their unique and colorful threads to the tapestry of my life.

I send warm thoughts and appreciation to all of the artists who continue to create beauty and offer their special talents to the world. I also thank the many art show vendors who were so generous with their help and advice, while I attempted to match their consummate ability to sell their art despite the challenges of weather, lack of customers, etc. They are a unique and hardy group who work together and assist each other in order to continue to achieve the status of being called "Art Gypsies."

Contents

1. Making the Decision……………………………………… 2
2. Moving to the Country……………………………… 6
3. Art on the Plaza, Monterey……………………… 8
4. Walnut Creek Art Show…………………………….. 14
5. Alamo Art Fair……………………………………. 20
6. Brookings OR, The Azalea Festival..…………… 26
7. Art in the Park, Morro Bay……………………….30
8. San Jose Fine Arts Show……………………………..36
9. Sale of Big Blue……………………………………..44
10. Give up yet?... 48

The Art Show Gypsy

The Art Show Gypsy

Chapter 1:   **Making the Decision**

My physician's diagnosis of mini strokes certainly caught my attention. I could hardly believe that at the age of 60, still feeling young and full of energy, a disabling stroke might be possible. I began to question what had happened in my life that could have brought me to the edge of a medical crisis. Perhaps it was my sometimes stressful forty-year career in management and accounting had caught up with me, or maybe it was surviving a difficult divorce after a 17-year marriage? I can't blame the kids because I never had any. Probably the real culprit was my consistently bad food choices, choosing inappropriate foods that elevated my moods, along with my cholesterol.

My current job as a controller for an assisted living corporation certainly caused me a lot of stress. Several years prior to my mini-strokes, I had resorted to taking Prozac to calm my A Type personality. My physician prescribed it for me after I expressed a desire to kill my micro managing supervisor. The shocked looked on my physician's face said it all. It was time for extensive therapy or medication and since it was an HMO, I was immediately placed on Prozac and left to fend for myself.

Within several weeks of receiving the Prozac, I was able to emotionally regroup and strategize an exit plan from my job. Fortunately several years ago I had made a real estate investment that had tripled in value during the "hot California Market" and I was able to reinvest the proceeds into a beautiful new home in the North State of California. I planned on spending the next year finishing the details on my new home, including landscaping the yard and preparing my condo for sale. My energy was consumed with shopping on EBay and the net for the perfect purchases for my new home. The landscaping project on the property was begun and many weekends were spent driving between my condo in Martinez and my home in Cottonwood. I had my condo kitchen remodeled, which was another huge project but well worth the effort as it really improved the condo for resale.

The Art Show Gypsy

Along with the dream of beginning a new life in my home in Cottonwood was the desire to change careers as well. I had spent over 35 years in the accounting field but my real passion was creating art. I had been painting in oils for over 20 years. I had participated in many art clubs and shows through the years and always looked forward to the day when I could really live fully as an artist. My new plan was to participate in the Art shows that were put on by promoters throughout California and the Southwest. What really appealed to me about my plans was the freedom of lifestyle it would provide me. I would no longer be chained to a desk or locked in a political dance with co-workers that I rarely had anything in common with.

I inched my way forward toward my final departure from my job and condo in Martinez. My condo was placed on the market and thanks to the kitchen remodel, it sold quickly. The closing papers were signed and I rented back from the buyer for several weeks while I completed the final details of my job and prepared to make the 3 hour drive north to Cottonwood. I could sense my supervisor's relief when I gave her my notice that I was quitting. She was as sick of me as I was of her. This was her opportunity to replace me with someone more in alignment with her personality, or lack thereof.

I purchased a van conversion to use in art shows. The van contained a full-size bed, along with a sink and refrigerator, as well as hot and cold running water. It even had a heater with a thermostat for use during fall or winter art shows. It was a Ford Econoline Van and was the largest vehicle I had ever owned. The top popped up to accommodate standing at the cook top or sink area. I named the vehicle "Big Blue" due to its midnight blue color and size. As a person who usually lived a conservative and pragmatic life, it was like setting sail for a new world and one that was rich in fantasy. There were a few flickering brief moments when the what-ifs began to surface but I dismissed the negative thoughts and continued to dream on.

My household was packed and prepared for the big move. I took my cats to the vet in Martinez to get their vaccinations. Travel cages were purchased for their trip north. The goodbye party at work was behind me. My boss deliberately snubbed me at the party, thus ending our dysfunctional four-year relationship. We didn't exchange addresses to keep in touch. I said goodbye to my special pals and my staff and wished them well and brought Big Blue to the office parking lot to show to everybody. My co-workers were pleased for me and wished me the best in my new home and career.

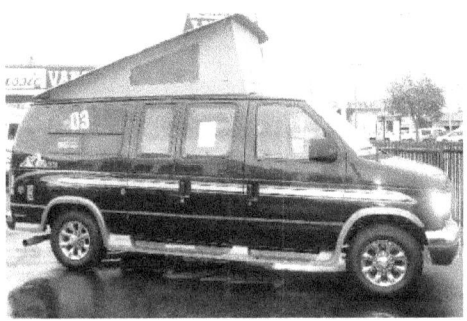

Big Blue Van Conversion

The Art Show Gypsy

Chapter 2: Moving to the Country

The move went smoothly with a wonderful family handling it. Despite the rainy day, they remained cheerful while deftly loading a multitude of boxes and heavy furniture into their sizeable moving van. I put the cats into their travel cages and when my household furnishings were packed in the van, we left for the three-hour drive to Cottonwood. The cats and I arrived safely late that night and slept on the floor awaiting the arrival of the moving van in the morning.

True to their word, the movers arrived early the following day. They unloaded all of my things and placed everything according to my specifications in my new home. After the movers left, I wandered around repeatedly thanking God for my beautiful new world. I stepped out on the deck and breathed the clean fresh air. In the distance Mt. Lassen, with a beautiful mantle of snow, was shining in the sun. I felt euphoric even with the pending chore of unloading all of the boxes and getting the household together. For the first time in my life, I didn't have to hit the ground running with a job to immediately report to. I could arrange my household at my leisure. Surely, I had died and gone to heaven, a feeling that unfortunately rarely lasts.

I met my new neighbor Francis and felt an immediate bond with her and her nice husband and son. Her contractor husband had built the house next door to me and they had recently moved in. Francis and I planned to join an exercise club together. Getting into better physical shape would be good for my health and help prepare me for the physical requirements of setting up shows. I've sat in an office chair for way too many years and the result was a definite expansion to my derrière.

I quickly settled into my new unstructured routine. The paintings were hung and the furniture arranged. The cats made their first foray into their new yard. Riley, my adventurous cat, was the first to go out on his mission of discovery. I'm sure he was amazed to find grass instead of asphalt. It must have been a relief for him to be free of dodging cars in a parking lot. The birds flocked to feed at the feeders I placed around the yard and they caught Riley's rapt attention. Holly, the female cat, slowly made her appearance outside. Initially she crept out on the deck with her belly close to the ground and only went a few yards but then she got braver with the sight of Riley chasing the birds in the yard. After several days she ventured out as far as the lawn and joined Riley chasing butterflies and bees. The cats were as happy as I was in our new country setting.

I spent January through March in preparation for my new career of participating in art shows. I painted new paintings and had Glicee' print reproductions made of them. I wanted to have an inventory of items that would range from inexpensive prints to expensive oil paintings. I applied all of the skills I had acquired in my business career to my own home-based business. I set up a separate artist bank account and purchased a hand held Visa machine that could handle sales transactions via a cellular connection. Other artists had told me about an artist's show guide which was published quarterly. The guide collected information from artists about the shows they had participated in. The publisher of the guide correlated the information received from participating artists and rated the shows accordingly. It also provided information about the promoters addresses and phone numbers so that they could be contacted about the shows. Planning well in advance was necessary in order to get accepted in a show. Pictures of my paintings and set-up had to be mailed to the promoter in order for them to decide whether you were to be included in their shows. After the review and acceptance from various promoters, my checks for space fees were cut from my new artist account and the forward momentum began!

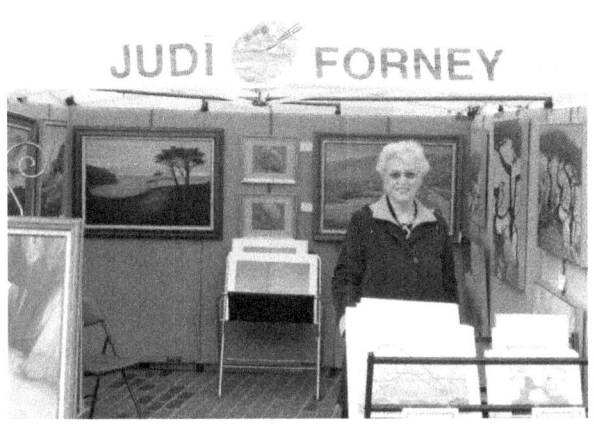

Chapter 3: The First show, "Art on the Plaza", Monterey

The first show was scheduled in early March in Monterey. I ordered a small 5 x 8 trailer in order to accommodate my Pro Panel stands and art inventory. That would allow me to use the van to sleep in and save on motel bills. The length of the van and trailer was over 26 feet, which was certainly well beyond anything in my prior driving experience. I ordered the trailer in January anticipating that I would have some time to practice driving with it attached to Big Blue. Unfortunately, the little Blue trailer arrived the day before the show in Monterey, so I had no time to practice and heaven forbid if I should have to back up. I could feel a cold sweat break out on my neck when I thought about possible scenarios with the trailer but my optimism carried me forward and I blithely assumed I could handle it. The Porta Potty was filled for just-in-case situations and put in the van. The next day I was off to Monterey with Big Blue and the small matching blue trailer attached with an iron umbilical cord.

My plan was to stay at a friend's home in Aromas, which is close to Monterey. Joe and Marion had built a beautiful Italian style home which resembled a villa. It was built on a knoll overlooking a small valley with a pond. The home was surrounded by rolling hills covered with old oak trees and it was truly an idyllic setting. Their home included a guest suite with its own separate entrance and that was where I would be staying. This should be a wonderful experience for the first show of the season.

Upon my arrival at their home, I was settled in the guest suite. Marion served a lovely dinner and we discussed the plan for the morning. Joe asked what time I would need to leave for Monterey. They provided me with an alarm clock so that I didn't miss my 5:30 a.m. wake up time. After dinner Joe was interested in seeing the van and trailer so we walked down to the cul-de-sac where it was parked. Joe appeared to be very impressed with the van and trailer set up and he provided me with his fireman's lingo that I had a nice "rig," a term I would use to describe my van and trailer from now on. He also made some helpful suggestions as to accessory items I would need, such as blocks for the trailer. It was nice to get a man's input for a change.

At first light in the morning I was off in my rig heading to downtown Monterey. I got rather lost in the maze of one way streets but knew I was in the right place when I spotted a line of vans on a side street. That has to be show people, I thought, and joined the long line at the end. When I got up to the front of the line I saw the entrance to the small city park was up and over the curb with a very tight right that veered around the street that was about twenty feet above the park. A city employee directing traffic came up to my window and loudly stated, "What are you doing here with that trailer?" I said, "I provided the promoter with the information in advance?" "I don't care; you can't bring the trailer down this way." "So where do you want me to go now and please don't tell me to back up." You will have to pull off to the left and follow the road around to the flat area of the brick park, over by the parking lot." I followed his instructions and weaved my way into the narrow space and found my assigned space on the exterior part of the show booths.

The rather poor space assignment on the outskirts of the show was due to my newly purchased trailer. I was learning lessons already. I hurried to start my set up but got hung up on the canopy and sand

The Art Show Gypsy

bags which weigh about 30 pounds each. The sand bags have to be attached to the canopy with bungee cords or there is a distinct possibility of doing a Mary Poppin's flying scene in the 30-mile-an-hour winds whipping across the Customs House Square. Another vendor helped me with the canopy and I dragged and attached the sand bags, then began unloading the Pro Panels and the rest of the paraphernalia and oh yes, the art work. An hour had passed between arriving at the square and getting the trailer unloaded. I was approached by the promoter to move my van and trailer immediately. I threw the rest of my artwork on the bricks of the Plaza and jumped into my van to start the engine but quickly discovered that I had left the headlights on and they had drained the battery. My 26 foot rig was completely dead and blocking most of the exit into the parking lot next to the square. Another vendor rushed to the rescue by jump starting the van engine and I was able to move it through the convenient parking lot to a very inconvenient lot designated for RV's and people dumb enough to haul a trailer to this event.

 I rushed back the great distance to my space to try to figure out what poles attached to what on my Pro Panels so that they could withstand the frigid wind and protect the paintings that were to be hung on them. Finally, in desperation the show director assigned someone to help me with the stand set up. I'm sure I didn't win any Brownie points with this promoter and hoped they wouldn't remember my name by the next show. It took me almost three hours to get my shop on the plaza set up and ready for business. It was at that point that the promoter came around to all of us to announce that due to the forecast of rain on Sunday, this would be a one day show, instead of two. Shoot I thought, I have to do double work today by having to set up and take down in the same day. I heard a lot of grumbling from the artists and vendors around me and we were all thinking the same thing, this sucks. The vendors around me said they were used to bad weather; it was just part of the business of selling on the street. The vendor next to me complained that he had driven over 9 hours in heavy traffic from San Diego in order to participate in this show. After much complaining and commiserating, we went back to our booths and waited for the customers to arrive. It was a long wait with just a scattering of customers on the square that day. The

The Art Show Gypsy

pottery vendor next to me did seem to snag the few customers that came to the show. I found myself wishing I had taken pottery classes instead of painting classes. It was already obvious to me that paintings and prints weren't the most useful purchase you could make compared to a plate or a coffee cup. I stood around all day resorting to eating fast food and running back and forth to the van to start it and run the engine so that I could leave the square that night. I didn't sell anything that day but the day went quickly and the show was over at five. I was still rather euphoric to be a part of the first show in my new career. The show promoter announced the show was over and the frantic take-down began.

     I rushed to the distant parking lot to get the rig to bring it back down to the square. Thankfully the engine turned over and I was able to join the parade of vans in line. This time I was fortunate to be greeted by a park employee who was a an earth angel and she helped me gain access to the congestion of the square. I immediately turned the engine off to conserve the battery while I repacked all of the paraphernalia from my booth. I ran around the plaza trying to collect all of the blue plastic card bags that had gotten away from me during a strong gust of wind. Around seven o'clock, I was ready to exit the square. I maneuvered the rig into the tight entry to the parking lot that I would have to pass through and exit. At the gate to the lot there was a ticket machine and although I wasn't going to park in the lot I had to grab the ticket in order to enter and raise the wood barrier blocking the entrance. I couldn't reach the ticket so I opened the door and stepped down to the curb to pull the ticket. My vehicle began to roll forward. I heard the snapping sound of the wood barrier and looked up in horror at the rear back up lights of a Mercedes backing out of their parking space right in front of me. I was hanging half-way in and out of the van door. I leaped back into the driver seat but in my panic I couldn't remember which pedal was the gas and which was the brake. The lights on the Mercedes got larger as they continued to back out of their space apparently oblivious to the impending doom rolling toward them. The momentum of the 26 foot rig was gaining speed. At last, I got my wits about me and stomped on the brake pedal. The Mercedes had pulled all the way out and went on its way, still unaware of its near miss with my rig. I picked up the broken barrier and threw it alongside the ticket machine.

      Horns behind me began to honk as they demanded to get into the lot too. My deodorant had definitely failed and I was sweating like a stevedore. I stopped at the gate as I was leaving to hand my ticket back to the parking lot attendant. I agonized over whether to tell him about breaking the wood barrier at the entrance but thought that since my motto as an artist was "Creating art that connects to Spirit", it would be better to be honest about it. After hearing my explanation he laughed and said he would call maintenance to replace the wood barrier and I was finally on my way. I stopped for Japanese food before returning to Joe and Marion's beautiful home. I hoped that the Miso soup would calm my nerves and warm my hands. After dinner I left for Joe and Marion's praying that the battery would turn over one more time and I would make it to their home. The engine started and I was off to Aromas, having narrowly survived my first show of the season.

      The day after the Monterey show was windy but clear as I left my friend's home in Aromas, for the five-hour drive north to Cottonwood. The big storm had apparently shifted east and missed Monterey. I could imagine the grumbling from my fellow vendors, since the show shouldn't have been cancelled after all. I chalked it up to experience and decided to list it in the "never again" category in my show planning journal.

The Art Show Gypsy

The Art Show Gypsy

Chapter 4: **Downtown Walnut Creek Art Show**

Fortunately I had plenty of time to rest and regroup from the rigors of the Monterey show, with the next show scheduled in Walnut Creek in April. Walnut Creek was close to my former home in Martinez, so I was very familiar with the area. I was looking forward to visiting friends during the show and possibly getting some help with set up and take down, as well as enjoying their company while we sat on the street watching people go by my booth.

I had high hopes that things would go more smoothly for the second show of the season. The weather had cleared, it finally stopped raining. I had done my homework completing several more paintings. Big Blue was gassed up at an ever increasing rate, making attendance at shows even more expensive. I was off for the three-hour drive to Walnut Creek.

At 7:00 a.m. I was standing in line with other vendor's downtown waiting to get my booth location. I nonchalantly shared with the promoter I hoped that I could unload my trailer on the public street. The promoter blankly looked at me and said "you have a trailer?" This was beginning to be a recurring theme. She suggested that I unload in the parking lot that was directly behind my booth space and then immediately move the van and trailer to the church parking lot. Since the church parking lot was located almost a half-mile away, I could envision that once again I would be hiking all over town because I had brought the "dreaded" trailer.

I pulled into the private parking lot and immediately began unloading. Strong winds were blowing along with the morning fog, so once again the heavy sand bags were an absolute essential part of keeping my panels in position. I hoped my paintings wouldn't blow off down the street, along with heaven knows what else. I certainly didn't want to have another ugly blue bag episode. My little shop on the street was easier to set up this time since I was more experienced. Then I was off to move my rig to get parked in the church lot. I stopped at one of the portable bathrooms on my way back to my booth, having already learned to never miss an opportunity for food, coffee, or use of a bathroom.

I made the 10:00 a.m. set up time designated by the promoters and now had a few minutes to meet my vendor neighbors. I was shocked to see that the artist next to me had an oxygen tank and her mother was hovering around her. Gina, who was the artist, explained that she had gotten out of the hospital the week before. She had been suffering from pneumonia. I wondered what her physician would say if he knew his patient was sitting on the street in the cold wind and fog. Gina had a rather sad assortment of small water color paintings displayed in a flimsy stand that continually fell over in the wind. I couldn't help but wonder what drives artists, including myself, to put them so at risk trying to get public approval? I left Gina with her oxygen tank and wandered over to meet the vendors on the opposite side of my stand. They were a cute young couple originally from India. I didn't catch their names because frankly I couldn't understand what they said. Later in the day when I was getting more accustomed to their somewhat challenging English, I found that they were an excellent source of art show information. They shared that they had been participating in art shows for the last two years. He did graphic art on his computer and together they created trivets and trays as well as some decorative pictures. How smart, I thought, to combine practicality with art. They commented that they were extremely unhappy with their location in the show. They felt we were too far out of the mainstream flow of the show, a remark that ultimately proved to be true.

The wind kicked up a notch in the afternoon and ripped the umbrella off my artist's chair. I watched it blow off down the street and was glad that I wasn't attached to it. The umbrella was retrieved by the Indian couple and returned to me. I couldn't imagine how Gina was holding up in the cold wind but she was still sitting there on a hard bench with her mother, continuing to breathe with the help of the oxygen tank.

At 6:00 p.m. our trial by wind was over and it was time to pack up the paintings and prints which, of course, required the van

The Art Show Gypsy

and trailer again. It was another day with no sales. I quickly walked the half mile to the church parking lot to get my van and drove it around to the street side location close to my space. Since the parking spots were vertical, there was no space for my 26 foot rig except the parking lot behind me. By this time on a Friday, the parking lot was full; the whole town was now full of people going to the nice restaurants and bars downtown. I pulled into the private lot and began to load the paintings and prints into the trailer. My friend Jen was helping me as we planned to go out to dinner that night. I heard a loud voice across the parking lot say "You had better get out of here, or I'm calling the police", so much for city of Walnut Creek's hospitality. I jumped back into the van and rushed out of the parking lot heading back to the church lot. Jen drove me back downtown for dinner at a nice Mexican Restaurant. Over Margarita's we discussed the day's events. Jen expressed her amazement at how much work was required to set up and display artwork. I mused "Perhaps, I need to find a strong man to assist me with the shows?" Jen said "What kind of fool would be interested in doing that kind of thing." I'm sure truer words were never spoken and proceeded to sip my Margarita and enjoy the food, happy to be in out of the wind and off the street.

  I spent the night parked by a friend's townhouse in Martinez. Elaine didn't have room in her home for me to stay but she offered to let me use her shower. I used her shower and after we spent some time together I wandered back out to my van, facing another early morning wake up call. I had always thought that Elaine lived in a nice quiet neighborhood but soon discovered that her neighbors were party animals. They partied and talked loudly throughout the night which kept me awake in my hard bed in the van. Even my earplugs didn't drown out the revelry. At 7:00 a.m. my small travel alarm awakened me to start the day. I dressed and washed my face and brushed my teeth in the van. So, this is the gypsy life I thought to myself. I was off to Mac Donald's for morning coffee and an Egg McMuffin.

  I parked in the church lot and again made the long walk to my booth. As I walked along the street I noticed that a lot of artist's stands had blown into the street. My panels were in disarray but the

The Art Show Gypsy

metal poles and sand bags managed to loosely hold them together. According to the vendor grapevine, some of the stands had blown over on high end cars the previous night. I smirked thinking that there was some divine justice in that, since people in Walnut Creek didn't appreciate or buy our art they can spend their money on car repairs instead.

Another long day loomed but at least the weather had improved. The gale winds had subsided and the sun was shining. Perhaps "today would be better" was my new mantra. The day proved to be longer rather than better, with another day of no sales. What was particularly frustrating was the number of people who whizzed by me without any notice of my paintings. There was no expense involved in looking and perhaps making a nice comment but people seemed too busy to take the time to do that. Vendors all around me were complaining about poor sales; the show doesn't measure up to prior years. The Art Fair guide owner was going to get an ear full about this show.

Once again it was time to pack up the paintings and prints for the evening. This time I was able to find a long parallel space along the curb about a ½ block away. I was kicking myself that I hadn't noticed it earlier but oh well; it will save me from being screamed at tonight. I threw everything into the Van and headed for my friend Christine's home in Martinez. Once again she had a full house but the driveway was available for my van and trailer. We had a nice dinner together and I was thanking my lucky stars for such wonderful friends. Friends who tolerated my current art show career and probably said under their breath, "I'm sure she will come to her senses soon." I was able to shower in Christine's house and plodded out to my van in my slippers with my toilet kit in hand. I settled in for the evening when, despite my stupor, the noise of the party across the street awakened me. I couldn't believe the bad luck of two neighborhood parties in a row. The noise went on all night while I tossed and turned. About 3:00 a.m. I couldn't stand it anymore and decided, "This is it, I'm pulling out of the show and going home." I splashed my face with cold water from the van sink then put on some lipstick and hit the road. I knew that there was security at the show, so I prepared my excuse as to why I was dismantling my stand

The Art Show Gypsy

a day early and leaving the show. This was definitely not a good thing to do as the promoter may not be inclined to accept me again in any of their shows. Another thing to consider was the expensive fee I paid in order to participate in the show. Exhaustion won the argument and I planned to blame my departure on my elderly father. I practiced the phrase, "Poor Dad, I wish that he would stop falling down and hurting himself." My phony excuse is prepared and I'm ready to leave the cold windy, no sales, show.

    I stopped for breakfast at Denny's and ran into a lot of people who were ending their evening just as I was starting my day. I had never had breakfast at 4:00 a.m. before so this was another first in my new adventure. I lingered over my Grand Slam since it still wasn't light and I would need some light in order to see what I was doing. I sipped my coffee and hoped that I would be awake by the time I reached downtown Walnut Creek. The light was beginning to break through in the eastern sky as I drove toward my booth. I arrived to empty streets and began to quickly load my stands and break down my displays. I felt like some sort of thief, stealthily loading my equipment. I noticed that the supposed security guard was nowhere in sight, so much for guarding my "stuff". I completed the dismantling around 6:30 a.m. and drove the two blocks where the promoter's booth was, along with all of their "favorite" artists. I'm learning the ropes of art shows now. New artist's who haven't shown with promoters before, get the worst locations in the show. I left them a note with the excuse of leaving due to my Father's fall. I indicated zero sales on the envelope they had provided me in order to obtain their commission on sales. The security guard finally appeared as I was dropping off my note at the promoter's booth. I gave him a brief explanation about my sudden departure and headed back to my van. I leaped back into my vehicle and headed north toward home. The sun was now shining over the horizon. I have to admit it was very exciting to cut and run. How truly out of character for the former controller who always followed the rules. What a discovery, breaking the rules can be fun!

    My eyes began to droop as I drove up Highway 5 heading for home. The stress, exhaustion, and lack of sleep for the last two days were catching up with me. The main traffic on Highway 5 was mostly Wal-mart and UPS trucks. I pulled into one of the rest stops along the highway and parked with all of the big Mack trucks. I pushed the art work off the bed, pulled the curtains shut and quickly fell sound asleep. I was even able to sleep through the loud sound of the generator on the truck next to me. It didn't matter; sleep was more pressing than loud noises at this point. I slept for several hours and awoke to start my journey toward home sweet home.

Chapter 5: Alamo Fine Art Show

Two weeks had passed since the last show fiasco and yet amazingly I was ready to go again. This show was going to be in Alamo, in an upscale neighborhood shopping center. Surely, this would be a better place to show my paintings? It was a smaller show than the previous one and was arranged around the open covered shopping mall. The artists were allowed to set up their stands the night before the three day show. My space assignment was wonderful, long and narrow, protected under the overhead eves and in a prime location. This was the Mother's Day weekend, so we all anticipated a lot of shoppers getting ready for Mom's special day. Safeway was just a half block away from where my booth was, so there should be a lot of traffic of shoppers going by me. Behind me was a wonderful French Bakery with yummy pastries and coffee. I felt very cozy and at home protected under the eve with plenty of space to spread out my pro panels and show the paintings in good light.

The vendor vans and campers were allowed to park in the alley behind the shopping center. The night I arrived, I splurged on a wonderful Thai dinner at one of the restaurants in the shopping center. After dinner I moved the rig around the back of the stores in order to park for the night. I discovered that quite a few vendors were already parked in the narrow alley in the back of the shopping center. However, there were two side by side parking spaces left, where I could put the trailer in one and the van in the other. The downside was backing the trailer into the space. The better part of the next half hour was spent trying to maneuver the trailer into the parking space. Finally one of the vendors took pity on me and he offered to help. He took the trailer off of the hitch and we pushed it into position into the space. We introduced ourselves and shook hands with greasy palms. His name was George and his specialty was wildlife art. I looked forward to seeing his work the next day but

The Art Show Gypsy

now it was time to crash as I had another big day ahead of me. It was rather hot in the alley, so I popped up the top of the camper to let in whatever cool air might be out there. What also filtered into my space was the sound of the generator of the vendors parked in an RV across the alley from me. They were cool and comfy in their RV enjoying the air conditioning and watching TV. The rest of us were sweating and silently cursing them for running the noisy generator. Around 10:00 p.m. I heard one of the vendors pounding on the offending vendor's door and stating loudly "turn that damn thing off". All was not well in the Gypsy encampment.

The bathroom facilities were in Safeway, which required a long walk through the store to the back where the restrooms were located. Well, at least it was better than a port-a-potty and there was hot and cold running water. I prepared for the day in my small little home away from home. I put on my make-up and dressed in the Chico's Travelers non-wrinkling clothes that I had purchased for art shows. I tried to look my best and attempted to look professional despite having spent the night in my van in an alley. This should be better, I thought, Safeway has a Starbucks. It takes so little to make me happy these days. I finished hanging my paintings and waited anxiously for the buying crowds.

In the absence of people on Friday morning, I was able to meet and greet my fellow vendors. George, the artist who had helped me with the trailer the night before came to visit my stand and asked me to join him for dinner that evening. I happily accepted, looking forward to dinner with him and an opportunity to glean some knowledge about art shows from a seasoned professional. His booth was custom made and had an overhang, so his customers didn't have to stand in the hot sun to view his work. It's funny the things you notice when you try something new. I really liked his realistic paintings of animals. George had done some nice black and white drawings as well. His work seemed to reflect the distinctive personality of each animal. George told me that this was how he made a living, painting and doing shows. Meeting someone who had been successful in this business gave me a sliver of hope.

Friday was very quiet and dragged on and I came close to falling asleep in my tall artist's chair. What awakened me was the

The Art Show Gypsy

vendor next to me. His name was Jacob and he was very energetic. I frequently overheard his sales pitch about the Corian boards he was selling and he appeared to be an excellent salesman. Jacob had whizzed in late on Friday morning and in about ten minutes had set up various wood cabinets that contained his inventory. The Corian cutting boards were shaped like animals, vegetables and fruit forms. We got to chatting in the absence of customers and I was soon to discover that Jacob's true passion was Goji Juice. Jacob talked about Goji Juice constantly for the next three days. He soon convinced me to taste the juice, as he continued with his spiel about the benefits of the juice. I sarcastically wondered how I got so lucky to have him as a neighbor. I thought that I had the perfect location until the subject of Goji Juice came up. His next ploy was to sign me up to sell Goji Juice. His enthusiasm about the juice allowed him to overlook the fact that I couldn't even sell my own paintings, never mind selling Goji juice.

    Thanks to the juice and whatever exotic herbs they contained, I was revived enough to start thinking about dinner with George. I was able to close up my Pro Panel stands by covering them with tarps. This saved me from hauling the paintings and prints back to the trailer tonight. George came by to talk about our dinner plans and said that he planned on using the BBQ attached to the side of his trailer which was parked in the alleyway. He would buy steak for our dinner and asked me to provide the bread and salad. I was rather surprised that we wouldn't be eating at one of the nice restaurants in the area but thought; this should be a different experience for sure. On my final stroll to the restroom in Safeway I made the purchase of ready-made salads and a loaf of French bread.

    I located George in the alley firing up his grill that did indeed flip down from the side of his trailer. He had set up a card table next to his trailer and apparently we would be dining alfresco in the alleyway. George had invited Pete, another vendor participating in the show, to join us. George grilled the steaks to perfection, and also cooked some asparagus in olive oil sprinkled with sea salt. George asked us to bring our own chairs as he only had one for himself. I brought my rickety guest booth chair and Pete brought an old wooden chair. I've heard of "bring your own bottle" before but never

The Art Show Gypsy

BYC (bring your own chair). I served the pre-made salad on the paper plates George had supplied for the occasion. The three of us perched on our mismatched chairs in the alleyway preparing for our gourmet dinner. Eating a steak on a paper plate was somewhat challenging, especially with a plastic knife but we were hungry and managed to eat it anyway. There were a few distractions when delivery trucks drove by emitting exhaust fumes but other than that dinner was enjoyable, in a weird picnic way.

    We all discussed what a moron the vendor was that kept running his generator but I think there was an underlying envy that he had A/C and TV while the rest of us didn't. Pete shared his story about the colorful seed packets that he was selling in his booth. Pete had discovered a chest in his Uncle's home in NJ after his Uncle died. In the chest were hundreds of the hand silk screened seed packets. I don't know when it struck Pete that this would be a great way to make a living, doing art shows and selling seed packets? I guess it was the appeal of the hippie lifestyle, as Pete obviously in his fifties still wore his hair in a long ponytail down his back. He traveled in an old antiquated RV that he said he purchased because it looked bad and he wouldn't have to worry about someone stealing it, or his precious stock of seed packets. Since Pete lived in a home in expensive Sonoma, I didn't think money was the issue. Obviously he didn't care if he or his vehicle looked ratty; he lived a lifestyle that he preferred. I would venture to guess that his seed packets out sold my paintings and prints. Pete's only concern was running out of inventory, while my inventory continued to pile up in my garage.

    George lived with his wife and daughter in the Sacramento area. George had been doing shows for over 25 years and said he made a living at it. He advised me that before the show he sent cards to his collectors in the area and as a result got a lot of repeat business. I'm beginning to get quite an education about the art show business but I was beginning to be perplexed after my recent experiences why anyone would want to make a living this way. I did notice that most vendors are in terrific physical condition, I guess all of that lifting and hauling pays off if you want to stay muscular and thin. Other than me, there were very few overweight vendors. You

The Art Show Gypsy

could certainly save money on gym memberships doing this for a living.

We were enjoying each other's company in our little table on the street, watching the sunlight fade behind the trees. It was then that the hordes of mosquitoes came out and started biting. Pete lifted up his paper plate to throw it in the trash and discovered that he had eaten part of his plate when he cut through his steak with the plastic knife. We all got a good laugh out of the huge hole in his plate. Everything was quickly cleared from the table with the onset of the mosquitoes and we all went back to our rolling homes for the remainder of the evening. Things were a little quieter since the generator was turned off earlier this evening, probably due to many complaints they must have received. The gypsy encampment slept fitfully in our various small trailers and RVs in the alleyway.

The next morning the rush to Safeway began, especially for the people who didn't have "self-contained" vehicles. My original love affair with Big Blue was beginning to diminish. No shower or toilet made it far less desirable.

Saturday and Sunday, my mood was elevated by several friends who came to visit. They were kind enough to watch my booth, so I could see the rest of the show and of course visit Safeway's restroom. Sales were minimal and certainly didn't begin to cover my expenses for the trip and show fee.

The take down was awful due to the heat and I sweated like a longshoreman while I packed up all of my stuff for the long drive home. It was a good thing I was traveling alone because I sure didn't smell fresh. Am I having fun yet? Nope. I had one last discussion with another artist who complained about his lack of sales, he told me that in the past he had sold up to $5,000, of his work in this show. We both wondered what was happening in the economy this year, 2006, that was responsible for the downturn in art sales? However, I noticed it was beginning to be a repetitive discussion that occurred at every show.

The Art Show Gypsy

The Art Show Gypsy

Chapter 6:   Brookings, OR., The Azalea Festival

A few weeks later it was time to pack up the paintings and prints into the trailer and head north to Brookings which is located on the southern coast of Oregon. Thankfully on this trip my friend Christine was coming along. She was always wonderful company and she offered to help with the set up and take down. We should have fun together no matter what happens. I have high hopes that this coastal city will be the right place to sell my ocean inspired art.

The views were awesome driving north toward Oregon on Highway 5. We passed the beautiful scenery of Shasta Lake and Mt. Shasta towered over us still wearing her mantle of winter snow. We stopped in Weed, CA. to see a Photographer. The photographer had done some Glicee' prints of my new oil paintings that I needed to pick up. Logic was telling me not to continue to add to an inventory that keeps going up instead of down but my heart keeps telling me that I'm going to be a success in this business, I'm just off to a slow start.

We left Highway 5, heading over toward the coast when the roads became much curvier and more challenging, especially when hauling a trailer. We arrived in Brookings after a challenging five-hour trip. The first sign of the Azalea Festival in Brookings were the tents being erected in the area of downtown. There was a slight drizzle of rain, which was certainly nothing new for Oregon and I was glad that my space was going to be in the high school gymnasium. Christine pointed out a sign that said "Craft Show" this weekend in the high school gym. "Craft show, I said?" I thought that I was going to be participating in a fine arts show. How did I miss that important piece of information in the Art Fair Guide? As we began to unload the trailer and haul my art into the gym, it began to be very clear that I was going to be an oddity in this show. Ever the optimist, I thought I should really stand out from the crafts participants in the show. They displayed the usual hand crocheted baby dresses, jewelry and small junky stuff you expect to see in a Craft show, with one major exception. There was a really fine

The Art Show Gypsy

sculptor in stone that was also participating in the show. He must have misread the Art Fair Guide too.

After unloading, I disconnected the trailer and left it in the far corner of the parking lot at the high school and Christine and I headed north on Highway One, looking for our motel. I had obtained the cheapest reservation that I could via booking a motel on the Internet. It was a shock when we actually saw the property. The room rental, despite the shabby accommodations, wasn't reasonable this weekend because of the Festival. Oh well, it's a legitimate business expense. I'm sure the IRS will love all my expenses with very little income on my future tax filing but I'll deal with that when it happens.

On Saturday, I went to work in my small booth in the middle of the craft fair. It was a rather claustrophobic location in the center isle of the fair. I attempted to create a gallery atmosphere by erecting my Pro Panels in a square shape and hoped the carpet covered panels would partially shut out the noise around me. On one side there was a craftsman who created intricate wood pictures and puzzles and on the other side was a jeweler. The sculptor several isles over could be heard talking loudly, obviously presenting his sales pitch to everybody that walked by. Wow, I hope I don't end up with that desperate quality trying to hype a sales pitch to sell my art. Shouldn't beauty just sell itself?

The first day of the show the weather wasn't pleasant, as it was raining heavily. I was glad to be in my small space inside where at least it was dry. Lots of people showed up for the "Crafts Fair" and obviously many of them were friends of the vendors as there was a very convivial, almost party atmosphere in the gymnasium. Crafts did appear to be selling and people took the time to look through my bins and admire my work. There were really lovely people running the show, as well as the visitors, but no sale remains a depressing no sale. I sat in my claustrophobic cubby hole for eight hours which was beginning to be a lot like my prior accounting work experiences. My friend Christine at least had the opportunity to buzz around the town in my van. I caught up on her day out in the "real" world. We went to the spaghetti feed held at the local Elk's Club and

The Art Show Gypsy

had a really good and inexpensive dinner, complete with cheap red wine which helped to elevate my mood.

The next day, the weather had cleared and Christine was off to explore the coast while I returned to my cubbyhole gallery waiting for the really big art sales to start. I was beginning to be envious of my friend because she had freedom and I didn't, the ball and chain of my art kept me tied to my small space. The sculptor was still talking loudly, attempting to entice people to buy his carved statues but I could tell his voice was getting raspy.

I continued to stick my head in the book I brought with me and looked up whenever a visitor ventured into my booth. The visitors were very kind but by the end of the show I had heard every possible excuse as to why they couldn't possibly afford to purchase my work. They seemed like hard working people who obviously didn't spend their money in frivolous ways. I started to put sales prices up on things but even my sales prices were beyond what they wanted to spend. The dulcet tones of the sculpture could be heard less and less as the day went on. I wondered if he was having the same experience as I was.

This time I had driven all the way to Oregon to learn another hard lesson. I did talk to another vendor in the show who had created small prints of lighthouses based on his original oil paintings. John said that he had some success marketing his paintings to light houses and galleries up and down the Oregon coast. John suggested that I try the annual arts fair out on the wharf where fine arts were featured. He said that he usually participated in the show and he thought it would be a much better show for me. This was more learning the ropes information but I wasn't ready to even consider it right now. It was rather like discussing when you want to get pregnant again, right after delivering your baby.

The crafts fair was over and I was given the opportunity to set up my canopy with other vendors in downtown Brookings. However, with no sales over the last two days I decided against it. Christine and I planned to go on a long hike along the beautiful Oregon coast instead. We reconnected the trailer to Big Blue and headed up the coast. I had recently read a Sunset magazine article about hiking the Oregon coast, so we followed their map and parked where they suggested and began hiking. It was so refreshing to be out in the air, enjoying the spectacular Oregon coastline. We hiked along a narrow trail and appreciated the wonderful smells of pine trees and moss, along with great views of the water and surf down below. We hiked several miles until we reached a waterfall that flowed gracefully down to the beach below. I was able to get some wonderful photographs of the area always thinking about future paintings. We returned by walking along Highway One to get back to the rig. Our hike almost made the trip worthwhile.

The Art Show Gypsy

Chapter 7: Art in the Park, Morro Bay

I had almost four weeks to regroup for this show. The show was over the 4th of July weekend and it would be another three-day show. I had to bring lots of books to read while I precariously balanced in my tall artist chair. If I was busy with sales then inactivity wouldn't be a problem. I could only imagine how joyful that would be.

It was good to be leaving Cottonwood for the coast, since the temperatures were soaring into the 100's. One day I stepped outside my front door and a wave of 118 degree heat hit me, it was like stepping into a blast furnace. I wondered if the high temperatures were doing any damage to my paintings and prints but decided that it would be too expensive to install air conditioning in the garage. I put a cool towel around my neck and headed out to the hot garage to repack my paintings and prints for the Morro Bay show.

The drive to Morro Bay took over six hours. I arrived around six and checked into a motel. My expenses were escalating with the increasing price of gas and motels. The motel I usually stayed in Morro Bay, usually in the fall, was much more expensive in mid-summer. I had tried to get into a campground and sleep in Big Blue but the campgrounds in the area were all full due to the holiday. I would definitely have to sell one or two paintings to recoup my expenses on this trip.

After checking into the motel, I drove up to the public park where the show was going to be held the next day. The area was already packed with other show participants and their vehicles and there wasn't any space at the curb. I would have to wait for early morning when the coast was clear in order to get set up. Meanwhile, I might just as well park my rig at the motel and stroll downtown for dinner at the wharf. I dined at my favorite restaurant that had a view of Morro Rock. I always found the rock to be very energizing and somehow I felt livelier whenever I was around it. That was fortunate, since I'll need a lot of energy again tomorrow. Between the wonderful view and excellent fish dinner, I was happy to act like a

The Art Show Gypsy

tourist and forget about the challenges I had ahead of me this long working weekend.

I was awakened at 6:00 a.m. by the motel wake up call. It was time to hit the ground running. Once again I drove to the park and this time I was able to pull into a parking space fairly close to my booth space. The unloading began and like the proverbial "ant with the rubber tree plant" I began hauling my stuff to my booth space in the center of the park. This time I thought that it would be easier to transport the heavy sandbags by using my metal art stand with wheels. I loaded up all four of the 30 lb. sand bags and began rolling the metal cart toward my booth. The weight of the sandbags collapsed the cart on the way to my space. My automatic instinct was to make a wild grab to catch the heavy bags. This movement almost jerked my left arm out of its socket. Oh great, now I'm going to be a one arm artist but at least it was my left arm, not my all important art creating right arm. Hopefully it won't be as noticeable as Van Gogh's missing ear.

My injury certainly increased the struggle of set-up but again my fellow vendors were kind and helpful. They got my canopy set up and the offending sand bags were attached so that it didn't blow off in the increasingly high wind. The fog also enveloped the area the previous night and the cool dark chill was pervasive, especially to somebody who was still adapting to the 100's inland. It took the usual 2 hours to haul all of the remaining stands, paintings, etc. This time I put down a small rug to complete the gallery look and feel to my small space. The rug thrown over the grass was to cause problems later in the show.

I moved my rig to a side street pretty far away from the show in order to accommodate the vehicles of the customers. I plopped down in my elevated artist chair with a cup of coffee in my still functioning right hand, while my left arm hung uselessly by my side. I was dressed for a winter day in Antarctica, complete with a wool coat, gloves and fuzzy hat. My lips had already turned blue and it became more and more difficult to communicate with anyone because my teeth kept chattering. A few hardy souls came out early that day, despite the cold weather. I assume they live in the area and their blood must be the consistency of thick catsup. I wouldn't recommend that they take a trip to Redding this summer. What really amazed me were the many bicyclists that ran through the fair whipping around people and art work. A bicyclist narrowly missed me as I was bent over hanging a painting and my butt stuck out into the sidewalk. Who knew some idiot on a bike would be riding on the sidewalk, particularly some moron wearing Speedo shorts in the freezing cold.

Trees in an art show are usually a vendor's friend but the huge old oak hanging right over our heads became our nemesis as the cold day unfolded. If it weren't for that darned tree we would be able to bask in a few rays of sunlight that broke through in the afternoon. My neighbor vendors and I all complained about the tree but nobody had the foresight to bring a chain saw with them. God knows we packed everything else. I'll have to put that on my equipment list for future shows.

Since very little was happening customer wise, I was able to get to know my neighbors. The neighbor across from me was a lady from the central valley and she was also unaccustomed to the cold weather. She and her husband sold decorated ceiling fan pull chains. She said her husband had set up a similar booth at another art show and they communicated with each other by cell phone from their separate locations. "That must be a fun marriage, competing on how many ceiling fan chains they each sold?" The couple next to me sold hand-made purses in a multitude of colors and fabrics and they appeared to be friends with the vendor located behind them. They spent most of the day in their lounge chairs laughing and joking with their friends. It reminded me of a tail-gate party before a ball game. Next to me were some nice ladies selling hand-made soy candles. Overall it was the usual group of hardy souls that participated in art shows. I ran into the nice Indian couple I had met in Walnut Creek and they were pleased that I followed their advice to participate in the Morro show. We all wished each other the best and returned to our booths to await the onslaught of buyers.

The highlight of this show for me, as usual, involved food. You could order lunch at a local deli and they would deliver it to you. Not surprising food continued to be one of my main interests, along with the question, "where are the restrooms located?" As the fog burned off and the sun broke through, except for those of us in the shade of the oak tree, people began showing up and browsing the fair. My neighbors appeared to be busy and I saw a few bags with purchased items in them, a sight that lends hope to the hopeless.

The long first day came to an end and I meandered back to the motel. I had sales of $200 which didn't cover my food or lodging for the day that I spent freezing my rear end off. Once again I placated myself by ordering pizza in my room and rented a movie. It was my means of escape to another world of artists who actually make a living at their craft. The grand finale was a hot shower and an attempt to defrost my left arm that still wasn't working since the accident in the morning. My sleep was fitful and I continued to wake up in pain every time I turned over and twisted my arm. I wondered how I was going to get all of that stuff back into the trailer with one working arm. Perhaps I could take a bus home, leaving my booth set up and paintings on the park lawn and hope it would all disappear. Would the Morro Bay Art Association sue me if I did such a thing? Those lovely thoughts took me away to dreamland.

My reflection in the mirror that morning was truly frightening. My once youthful good looks had already faded with age but now the image of a crone' stared back at me. Perhaps haggard would have been a better description. I had always prided myself for not having bags under my eyes but the bags were there this morning and they were totally over-packed like my luggage consistently was. I'm beginning to be concerned that at one of these shows I may drop dead of exhaustion in my booth. What was I thinking when I embarked on this misadventure? I had better drink the awful coffee in the motel room before I head out the door for the park and that darned tree. My mood was quickly going downhill, no wonder I rarely sell anything. Perhaps making sales aren't my greatest personal strength? Ya think?

The next two show days were pretty uneventful and passed quickly except for a few minor episodes. A very nice lady was visiting my booth and as she stepped inside she caught her heel or

The Art Show Gypsy

the rug that I had put down to complete the gallery impression. Fortunately I managed to catch her before she crash landed in the middle of my booth. As timing is everything in life, one of members of the art club monitoring the fair was passing by at the same time. I was admonished to take care of the problem with the rug before anyone got hurt. I used some duct tape on the rug and tried to adhere it to the grass but that didn't work. I thought duct tape worked on anything but I guess not. The rug is staying because I'm not going to haul it to my trailer before the end of the show. Only my stubbornness is keeping me going now.

The weather continued to be foggy and cold in the morning with high winds in the afternoons. The usual comments from vendors all around me was "sales are down from last year". Wow, I guess I really missed out; I should have started doing this last year. Oh well, it's too late to change that now. I did have the support of my fellow vendors who encouraged me to try other shows where my fine art might be more successful. One of them suggested a show at Fort Mason in San Francisco but I can't even bring myself to think about driving my rig in the city. A happy thought did cross my mind; I could leap off the Golden Gate Bridge on the way out of town, if sales continued to be as bad as they have been so far.

Actually I was no longer receptive to planning future shows, having barely survived the latest flop. The time had come for the arduous task of my one-armed take down. I started by packing the paintings and framed prints in their boxes and began the long wait for the opportunity to get my rig closer to my booth space. There were very few people left in the park when I began hauling my stuff to my trailer that was inconveniently parked on the other side of a busy street. It was difficult to carry the panels and still be able to see the oncoming traffic; I thought go ahead run over me, make my day.

However, God smiled down upon me and provided me with a large family who just happened to be at the park and they amazingly offered to help me. I blessed the Dad of this crowd of kids and silently thanked him for his sex drive which had provided so many helpful children. It was one of the rare occasions that I considered that not having kids might have been a serious omission in my life

The Art Show Gypsy

but it's far too late to dwell on that now. The kids and their kind Dad all started packing my stuff to my trailer. Motorists on the busy street even stopped to allow the children to cross safely to the other side where my trailer was located. The reality that there are indeed some very kind people in the world made my heart glow on the long drive home to Cottonwood.

    The next few weeks were spent soaking my arm in an attempt to recover use of it. This was particularly important because my next show in San Jose, just a month away. I doubted I could count on another large family to be around to help me again. I was really excited about the final show of my 2006 season. I had attended the San Jose Art show twenty years ago and had been very impressed with the quality and diversity of the artists who had shown their work at the show. Now it was my turn to show my work with other artists and my last shot this year to actually make some money in my long dreamed of art business.

Chapter 8:   San Jose Fine Arts Show

I hoped that my art show season would end on a high note, one that would motivate me to continue to create art at home through the cold winter months. I tried to make reservations at a RV park in San Jose but was rebuffed by the person on the phone after she asked if my RV was self-contained. Why yes, I responded, "I have a Porta-Potty". Apparently that was the wrong answer because she said, "We don't accept vehicles that don't have built in toilets since we have had too many bad experiences with people dumping their Porta-potty on their grounds of our park". I said, "Why, that's totally gross, I wouldn't do that". "Never-the-less", she said, "that is our rule and we can't accept you in our park." What a shock, RV discrimination, that's a first. My romance with Big Blue had really faded, where I once saw perfection, I was now living with the flaws. The flaw this time meant I had to pay big bucks on a motel again. I made my reservation at a motel close to the light rail in downtown San Jose and hoped that they would have space for my 26' rig.

I left Cottonwood around noon for the four-hour drive to San Jose. I reviewed the long list of instructions provided to me by the promoter of the show. The set up in downtown would be after 9:00 PM. The police would have to close off downtown streets in preparation for the show that featured over 400 vendors along with musician's stages and food vendors. It was Friday and they would have to clear the streets of traffic which would take quite a bit of time, thus the late set up time.

I checked in the motel and discovered that there was no space to park Big Blue and my trailer in the very small parking lot. I proceeded to drive around the area dodging downtown traffic, until I spotted a large hotel behind my motel where I would be able to park the van and the trailer together. It just required that I drag my luggage across the street to the motel where I was actually staying. I hoped that the hotel wasn't checking the license plates of their guests and that my rig wouldn't be hauled off in the middle of the night by the police. I would be a no show if my vehicle and trailer were

The Art Show Gypsy

impounded. I wondered if I could get my $400 fee back. Great, I really needed something else to worry about.

I checked in the motel and discovered that my room was just outside the door of the motel reception area. It was an enclosed area surrounded by concrete, where the main traffic flow would occur, something that became very clear later that day. I went to the motel lobby and found a nice restaurant and proceeded to have a leisurely dinner. It was the calm before the storm and once again it was food that saved the day. No wonder I'm plump.

I went back to my room to settle in for a while before preparing for my departure to downtown. The sound of skateboards outside my room began to be deafening. The kids were actually using the sidewalk as a skateboard park, whirling around the area screaming and yelling. The noise level from the pool which was also close by was also reaching higher and higher decibels. Well, this was the Labor Day weekend so I guess I should have expected it to be noisy. I imagined that the kids' parents had rented rooms for them and then dropped them off for the long weekend. I assume the parents then returned home to peaceful, kid free, houses. I guess it's a good thing I'm not a mother with that kind of thinking. This was going to be one heck of a night. Now I'm really sure that I'm too old for this insanity; I should have tried the art show circuit thirty years ago or better yet, not at all.

I drove Big Blue toward downtown but wasn't sure about which exit to take. The sun had set and it was completely dark now. I managed to miss the right exit and had to circle around the city again. This time I could see a line of vans, trucks and RV's on the city streets below the freeway. The police had barricades and roadblocks on all of the city streets. This was really going to be a challenge getting to my booth space.

I followed a long line of vendors snaking their way to their booth site and discovered that once again, I couldn't get very close to my space. This time a large truck had blocked my access. The night air was invigorating and it helped to energize me so that I could begin set-up. The vendor next to me helped me to erect my canopy and I'm always relieved to get that done. My left arm still

The Art Show Gypsy

wasn't fully recovered from the Morro Bay episode and this trip my back decided to not co-operate either. Daydreams of hot baths and massages kept me going. I became a blur of activity limping back and forth between my space and trailer. Fortunately I had purchased a small piece of moving equipment with wheels that folded up so I could transport my sand bags and boxes on it. On the street, small things mean a lot. My display stand that had collapsed under the weight of the sand bags in Morro Bay now had a bent frame and lurched crookedly to the right. I felt as though my body and the display frame were a close match, as both of us were bent out of shape. All I needed now was an oxygen bottle and I would right on par with the artist in the Walnut Creek show, and I thought she was crazy? Now I know who's really crazy. I should be back on my anxiety medication but I don't have health insurance anymore and I can't afford it. My mind's wandering, I really need to get focused and unload this stuff.

    The big truck that had originally blocked me when I arrived had finished setting up and had left. This created a large opening in the space in front of my booth space but I had to go all the way around the block to reposition my rig. You know the drill; I still can't back up the trailer. Off I went back around the block through police road blocks at midnight on now much quieter city streets. I had noticed the orange cones blocking the left hand lane on the street on the way in and had gone around the block on my first approach but this time since traffic was so quiet, I decided to make the left hand turn anyway. In my blurry eyed state who cares about a few cones? I proceeded to make my turn and was stopped at the police guard rail. The security guard at the gate immediately began screaming at me, "Do you know what you just did?" Uh yes, I stupidly replied. I smiled like an Ingénue and hoped that he would stop yelling. He stated "You have deliberately driven across a street that the police blocked off with cones." "There was an accident here earlier this evening between a vehicle and the light rail because someone had done the same stupid thing that you just did." He then called a police officer over to my window. I thought, "Oh, oh, I'm really in trouble now". I wondered just how expensive the ticket would be, or worse yet would I be spending the night in the jail? The officer read me the riot act and threatened to issue a ticket. I just kept

The Art Show Gypsy

apologizing for my gross stupidity and promised that I would never do that again. I thought that since the officer didn't actually know me, he might believe what I said. However, I knew that I'd spent my whole life doing stupid things and I'm pretty sure it wasn't going to end tonight. When the officer's tirade was over and I was thoroughly admonished for not following police instructions, he released me to finish my set up at 1:00 a.m. Perhaps the officer took pity on me because I looked like his grey haired mother, or maybe he knew only a complete idiot would be out on a public street setting up an art booth in the middle of the night.

I completed my set up and luckily there weren't many people left to see my red face from the episode with the police. My blood pressure must be totally out of control by now. I covered the panels with large plastic sheets and used clips to hold them in place. The vendor next to me was going to spend the night in his RV in front of his space and he said he would watch out for my stuff. I wished I had thought of spending the night there too, probably the middle of the street was quieter than the motel but then we get back to the Porta-Potty issue, darn.

I arrived back at the motel which still had quite a few revelers celebrating. Thank God it's Friday and a long weekend too. With my exhaustion, noise was no longer an issue for me. I passed out on the hard bed still fully dressed and slept like I had one foot in the grave, which I did.

The morning dawned bright and clear, which is always a good thing when you are going to spend the day exposed to the elements. I decided to take the light rail into the center of the city, since all of my work was already in my booth. I passed by Big Blue parked in the other hotel parking lot, to make sure it was still there and I looked for a ticket in the window. Thankfully it was there with no ticket. I proceeded to walk to the light rail, dragging one leg because my sciatica had really kicked in big time. I just hope I have the fortitude to make it through this grueling weekend.

The light rail was a pleasant ride and it only took a half hour to get into downtown and my booth space. I surveyed other vendor's booths on my way into the show and noted that there didn't appear to be much actual art. The vendor on my left was Chinese and had clothing that had obviously been made in China, the main clue being the labels that said "Made in China" on each garment. The vendor on my right sold hats that had undoubtedly been made in Mexico. Since everything displayed in the show was supposed to be handmade by the participating artist, I wondered about the breakdown in quality control by the promoters. Oh well, I need to get my art displayed in my small gallery booth. The subject would come up again from other artists in the show.

The booth location was excellent since there would be music and bands playing directly across the street. Food booths were at the end of each section of street and there were plenty of portable potties throughout the show. The show had advertised an attendance in the thousands and true to their word, lots of people began showing up. I did notice that people in my direct vicinity were busy trying on hats and the hand beaded Chinese capes that my neighbors were selling. I had my share of visitors and received a lot of kind comments about my art but not many sales. I kept repeating my mantra, tomorrow will be better. My step-mother had once told me that I reminded her of one those plastic inflatable dolls that had weights on the bottom. You could punch the doll and it would come right back up. It's ironic how your childhood resurfaces when you're under stress. Here I am so many years later, still being punched and yet still popping back up. Perhaps a strand of perseverance must be in my DNA.

I stayed open late that evening to enjoy the entertainment and be open for shoppers after the show was over. As usual I placated myself by indulging in the many food booths in the area. The entertainment was over by nine and I was back on the Light rail heading back to the motel. Things were a little quieter at the motel as I'm sure a lot of people had complained about the noise on the prior evening.

The weather continued to be excellent the next day of the show and riding the light rail worked out really well. The promoter provided staff to help the vendors and as a means of communicating with the staff the vendors were each given a red clothes pin to

The Art Show Gypsy

display on the front of our canopy when we required a break. Undoubtedly I put up my red clothes pin more than they would have liked but it did provide me with an opportunity to see the rest of the show. I began my fast stroll around the streets and was amazed to see that most of the vendors were not selling art, just lots of tee shirts, junky pottery and things that were obviously not handmade. It seemed like only 10% of the show actually had artist/vendors with their own hand made art. I felt that the show had slipped precipitously in the last twenty years and the emphasis was no longer on fine art and sculpture.

Handmade or not, I proceeded to spend my money like everyone else on jewelry and several sequined Chinese capes for an upcoming cruise, as well as pottery and sweatshirts. My expenses continued to mount in my non-profit business. However, my mood remained irrepressible as I continued to remind myself, this is my last show for the year, and I might as well enjoy it.

After my latest jaunt around the complete show, I happily nestled back in my artist chair munching on kettle corn. One of my fellow artists, John, burst into my booth and began complaining loudly about the lack of actual fine art in the show. To prove his point John grabbed me by the arm and dragged me out to the center of the road, as I proceeded to spread a trail of popcorn all over the street. He said look at the vendors around you, it's nothing but Buy and Sell, a term I had never heard before. He said, "How are you supposed to sell art in this environment?" I thought, "oh good," his statement provides me with a legitimate excuse to give my friends. John continued to rant about the lack of artists in the show and he told me that he had called the San Jose Mercury newspaper to report that there was no fine art in this fine art show. He said that a reporter was coming to meet with him to do an interview about the show. John continued to rage and said they should call this a flea market or swap meet but not an art show. It was obvious to me, since I no longer had Prozac medication to offer, it was beyond my ability to calm him. I could only wish him well in his interview, as well as his future in art. After the experiences I've had this year I've come to the conclusion that with the advent of the computer and Internet, there have been many changes that have had an adverse affect on

The Art Show Gypsy

actual living artists. The idea of buying expensive original art on the street had lost its appeal to the public. Less expensive graphic arts could be obtained on the Internet and the new digital cameras meant you could create your own art and then print it on your printer at home. My assessment was that families today attend art shows for the entertainment and food and for a day of fun in the sun together.

When I fully mulled over my conclusion of today's art market and the experiences I've had over the last seven months. I made the decision to not continue doing street art shows. The positive aspects of the art show life had been meeting the wonderful vendors and artists who continue to persevere in the face of adversity by creating art and sharing their work on public streets. I know now what true warriors they are but I've also learned about myself that despite my false bravura; basically I'm a cream puff. It was time for the old gal to go home and let go of the dream of being an art show gypsy. Having made that major decision I was able to relax and to enjoy the rest of my last show.

Overall the show was very positive for me because I really enjoyed the visitors to my booth and their kind remarks about the quality of my art. I think the public appreciated that they would be seeing fewer of "my kind" in future shows. Sales totaled $300 for the three-day show and didn't even cover the purchases I made from fellow vendors. The final hours dragged by sitting in the hot sun waiting for the final take down. I made my last bathroom run and drank another cup of coffee and the show was finally over. I advised my fellow vendors that I would be back in an hour or so, as I had to take the light rail back to my vehicle. They were busy packing and loading their stuff so one less person in the mix worked for them. They promised to keep an eye on my things as I headed for the light rail.

Thank heavens my rig was waiting for me in the hotel parking lot and there wasn't a ticket on the windshield, what a lucky break. I took the driver's seat in Big Blue and brought her around to go back downtown to pick up my stuff. The traffic of people leaving the show and over 400 vendors trying to get out was horrendous.

The Art Show Gypsy

This time, I made sure to follow police instructions as I patiently waited my turn to approach my booth.

The hat vendor, Stan, helped me take down the canopy and I commented how I hated the darn thing. Stan immediately pounced on my remark and asked if he could have the canopy. I hesitated for one instant and then said yes, take it, I wouldn't need it anymore. He immediately began stripping off the letters of my name from the face of the canopy. I was relieved that the letters came off as I had feared that people seeing my name might think I had gone into the hat business. The Chinese Vendor, Lilly, noticed I gave Stan my canopy and she eyed my expensive dove grey Pro Panel stands and asked if I would be selling those? She probably fantasized she could get them for ten cents on the dollar. I said, "No Lilly, I will be keeping those" (I could always hang laundry on them). After getting everything packed I turned Big Blue toward home feeling lighter and freer than I had for a long time.

The ride home was uneventful and the next day my neighbor Bill, a former truck driver, helped me by backing the trailer into my garage. Bill asked me, "So how did the show go?" I responded, "don't ask" and quickly closed the garage door to retreat to my bed.

Chapter 9: Sale of Big Blue

It took a long period of recuperation to physically and mentally recover from my art show experiences. I needed many chiropractic adjustments to get my back into alignment again. My arm finally healed many months later, proving to me again how amazing and resilient the body is. My thoughts however, were a more complex challenge to fix. I was deeply disappointed by my inability to sell my art and it created a block, which stopped me from creating new art. What was the point? It was time to figure out another game plan for making a living in the coming years.

The best thing for me to do now was to figure out my immediate financial requirements. My bank account had perilously descended after all of the art expenditures of the last year. The final result of my cash assessment was that Big Blue would have to be sold. I researched the current value of the vehicle and discovered the dealership had over-charged me for the van last November. Oh well, it was too late now to get upset about it. I just marked it at the much lower Blue Book price and began advertising it in the local papers. I also listed it for sale on various web sites on the Internet. I received some totally absurd offers from the Internet ads which I chose to ignore, since thankfully I wasn't desperate yet. After a few weeks, I decided to run a more expensive ad in the local paper featuring a picture of Big Blue with the top popped up. Happily the new ad worked and I received some responses. One of the calls was from a lady named Edith. I noticed that her voice was a little shaky and she sounded like a senior citizen. The other call was from a man named Cody. Cody couldn't see the van right away but he would call me when he was available. My imagination immediately kicked into high gear. I could envision a tall handsome cowboy in tight jeans and a western hat. Was this my opportunity to finally meet a cowboy in Cottonwood? The reality check was when Edith called back to make an appointment to see the van on Friday morning. Sure I could meet her but the thought flickered across my mind that showing her the van would be a total waste of my time.

The Art Show Gypsy

Cody called back to make an appointment the same day and I told him about meeting Edith Friday morning. I didn't think that I would be too long with Edith then I would drive to meet him at the new Super Wal-Mart parking lot in Anderson. I washed Big Blue for the last time in preparation of her sale. The midnight blue paint sparkled in the morning sun; she was as ready as I could make her for her next appointment with destiny.

I headed off to meet Edith in a local shopping center. I spotted her as soon as I drove into the parking lot. She was a rather frail looking elderly lady holding tightly onto her daughters arm. They recognized my van by the color and for sale sign in the window. She waved me to park in a location close to them. Edith walked slowly over to the van and I wondered why on earth would she be interested in buying an RV? Despite my wonderment, I immediately launched into a show and tell of all of the accessories included in Big Blue. I managed to throw my back out again, trying to get the back seat down to show the off the full size bed. I hoped that I could stand in an upright position when I met Cody.

I offered Edith the obligatory test drive and surprisingly, she accepted my offer. It took her at least ten minutes to back the van out of the parking space. I was beginning to panic and twitch in my seat. Edith finally got out of the parking space and soon we were driving down a country road close to the shopping center. She began to share her life with me as she drove. She had lived in the Sonoma area most of her adult life and her career had been in nursing. She had been widowed fairly young and had raised two daughters by herself in their home in Sonoma. Her children had grown up and moved away and Edith had subsequently retired from nursing. When she visited one of her daughter's in the beautiful community of Weaverville, she really liked the area and decided to move there. She sold her home in Sonoma and as a result had a nice nest egg to purchase a modular home that she loved in Weaverville. Unfortunately, soon after Edith moved into her new home her daughter's husband lost his job and they had lost their home. Edith allowed them to move into her modular home. They both smoked which created a polluted atmosphere in her home, this prompted her to begin spending her weekends touring parks in the area and staying overnight, usually

The Art Show Gypsy

sleeping in the open back of her Toyota pickup. Several weekends ago she said that a bear came into the campground where she was staying and ripped into her cooler and ran off with it. The cooler had been left on the picnic table fairly close to where she was sleeping in the back of the Toyota. I seized my opportunity to push the point that it would be much safer for her in an enclosed vehicle like Big Blue during her camping trips. I'm sure it was a conclusion she had already reached and that's why she was looking at the van. Edith and her other daughter had planned a trip to San Diego in a couple of months and she wanted to make sure they both would be safe and protected during their trip.

After we talked for awhile it dawned on me that I had met a kindred spirit in Edith. She had the same unsinkable character as I did. Edith was impressed with the van and said, I think I'll buy this. How much did you want for it? I mentioned the full sales price and she agreed to pay it. I thought I would be overcome with giddiness and almost passed out in my seat. We returned to the shopping center where her bank was conveniently located. She handed me a cashier's check for the full amount and right there in the parking lot the van was sold. It's amazing how easy things are when God makes the arrangements. I've spent so much time in my life twirling and spinning, attempting to make things turn out the way my ego wanted it. From here on I will make every effort to live by the motto "Let Go, Let God," well at least for the next week or so.

I immediately called Cody and cancelled our appointment telling him I had sold the van. I still hoped to meet a cowboy sometime but this day was committed to a lady who lived life full throttle as she continued to create a colorful life for herself, despite her age and health issues. I hoped to mimic her one day.

I needed a ride home since they were taking the van, so we had one last ride together and I got to hear more details of Edith's life. She told me that she had a stroke several years ago which was why walking was difficult. At the time of the stroke she also lost her ability to speak clearly. The doctor doubted that she would regain her full ability to speak but she chose her own homeopathic remedy and took up playing an Australian instrument called a didgeridoo.

The Art Show Gypsy

Being a former nurse she knew that playing the instrument would stimulate her cheeks and lips and help her regain her speaking ability. Edith now plays the didgeridoo and also speaks clearly. I was transfixed with her story and thought she definitely qualified as one of the more interesting women I had ever met. After she and her daughter dropped me off at home, I watched her drive off in my cherished van. I wished her, "God speed Edith," I hoped she would enjoy many trips to the wilderness, safely contained in "Big Blue."

The Art Show Gypsy

Chapter 10:   Give up Yet?

Despite my determination to not do anymore shows, I decided to participate in just one more show at Lake Almanor, sponsored by Plumas Arts. The show was about an hour and a half from where I live and I still had my small blue trailer to haul my art; although I would have to add a trailer hitch to my Van in order to haul the trailer. The art fair was to take place on Collins Pine Meadows, a large park covered by lawn and protected by large pine trees all around the park. It was another three day fair, so I would have to stay in a motel for two nights in order to get my set up done early and meet the required show times.

I arrived early on Friday morning and began the arduous task of set up. I really liked the members of Plumas Arts, who were organized and really helpful to the myriad of artist/vendors who were participating in their show. They also had their children and local boy scouts assist us in getting our stands set up. I was immensely relived to get help, especially since my designated site was in the middle of the large grassy park which looked flat from the edges but contained quite a few lower spots, which I discovered while hauling the dreaded sandbags across the grass. I hit a low spot which I would describe as a Buffalo wallow, although I never saw the Buffalo. Everything on my cart fell off into the grassy hole. The Boy Scouts were to the rescue, picking everything up and re-loading it onto the cart for the rest of the journey to my space.

They also helped me to set up my new canopy, which contained an awning that projected out from the top, to protect the front side of my display panels from the sun or anything else that the weather Gods produced. I began hanging my work and completed the set up by the time required by sponsors. After all the effort of the morning all I wanted to do was lay down in the cool grass and just enjoy the day, however, once again it was business as usual and the reason for all of my effort was to "sell art." I plopped myself down in my tall chair, purchased specifically so I could look people in the eye without having to stand up every time someone entered my booth. I did have a few minutes to cruise the show before the opening of the

The Art Show Gypsy

show and was very pleased to discover that I was surrounded by artists and craftspeople that had wonderful, high quality goods to sell. This should be a good show I thought, ever the unsinkable optimist.

Well, the weather was sunny and mild, however, my usual concern was "where are the buying customers?" I did take a few moments between visitors to talk to a fellow artist located close to my booth, I wanted to get her perspective of this particular show. The watercolor artist shared that she has done well in the past participating in this show however, sales this year had been pretty slow so far. When I noticed that some of her prices were in the range of $2,000 and up, I felt like erecting a sign with an arrow to my space indicating, "Cheap art, for sale two booths down." On the final day of the show she did sell one of her expensive paintings, which made the whole effort worthwhile for her. Once again I had total sales of around $200, framed prints and cards but wait I haven't gotten that far yet, the shows not over and I'm still in the wishful thinking phase.

Plumas Arts hired security for the event, so after the show was over that day, I put up my plastic panels to cover my paintings and blocked the front of my stand from being easily entered. I seriously doubted someone would go to the trouble of trying to steal art I couldn't sell but you never know some crook may have unique taste. I drove back to the motel to turn in for the night with the adage, "another day another dollar" floating through my head.

I went to my hotel room and discovered it was one of the smallest rooms I had ever stayed in, not the cheapest, but definitely the smallest. The walls were covered in pine planks making if seem like I was a squirrel living in the dark hole of a tree. The room was dark and rather warm, so I opened the windows to let some air in. After several house of watching television, I noticed that there were quite a few people out on the patio and around the pool who were talking with each other. I stuck my head out the door and noticed they seem to be other artists and vendors from the show. Since they were all so chummy I got the impression it might have been an annual event for them to get together.

The Art Show Gypsy

I should have been more social and joined them but I was tired so I took a shower and got into my jammies, getting ready for another action packed day tomorrow. I noticed that the noise level outside had increased and a unique smelling smoke was now filtering into my motel room window. If I wanted a cheap high from someone else's pot, I could keep the window open but I wanted to be fresh for the morning, so I closed the window and turned on the room sized air conditioner which helped to filter out the smoke along with the noise. This is what I meant about getting into this business too late in my life, if I had been younger I definitely would have joined the party and would be tossing down glasses of wine with the rest of them. I seemed to have turned into a party poop, perhaps from too many years of living a solitary life? Maybe I'll pick up my second wind when I move into Assisted Living and my fellow seniors are all on drugs, (not the good kind) perhaps Pot will be legal by then and I can indulge, as usual projecting a fantasy ending on my thoughts.

The next morning I was up and out early and the chatty crowd from the night before was slow in awakening. I bought coffee and a pastry before going to man my booth in the middle of the meadow. Again we were blessed with a lovely day and no wind. I thoroughly enjoyed spending the day surrounded by pleasant people and being able to talk about my art with the special people who actually took an interest in it. The weather and the people were encouraging but I finally came to terms with the reality that this would be my last show, really, I mean it this time.

The evening was a repeat of the night before and once again I decided to stay in my little squirrel den, in lieu of joining the crowd around the pool. Perhaps my conservative concern about someone calling the police may have influenced my decision, or perhaps a lifetime of living around the edges of society, was a more natural choice for me. Since this was the last night for the show the party rocked into late night hours, however, my formula for sleeping, exhaustion along with the sound of the A/C served me well and I was able to sleep most of the night. In the morning I attached my trailer to my Van and headed over to the show. Another long day ensued with very little sales and finally the time came to pack up and leave. A wave of Boy Scouts arrived to "save the day" and help me

The Art Show Gypsy

get all of my stuff across the lumpy meadow and back into my trailer. Tapping into my cash box, I fished out dollars to pay them with and also handed out packets of my art cards to the really hard workers. It wasn't until later that I realized I had given them cards with "Dancing in the Wind" picturing a nude dancing in the clouds. Undoubtedly their mothers weren't too pleased with that particular image but oh well, I'm an artist and we think visually and invariably fail to make the connection with most people's reality.

I'm back home now with my angel pets living a peaceful, albeit boring life. I've come to terms with the reality that I'm not included in the two percent of working artists who actually make a living creating art. With those odds I'm surprised anyone would even attempt a career in art and frankly it even makes me glad that I spent forty years in accounting and management where my work actually generated an income. Had I started in my earlier years, I may have ended up like Van Gogh, missing an ear or worse yet shooting myself in the head. I comforted myself with the fact that Van Gogh only sold 4 paintings in his lifetime and look at the price of his work now. My only remaining art fantasy is that after I'm dead my art will be discovered and will finally be appreciated for its unique style of rendering. Then reality strikes and I realize that's just my ego talking, undoubtedly when my family cleans out my house they will call 1-800 got junk and have it hauled off.

I put my little blue trailer up for sale and sold it quickly to a local contractor, it had hardly been used and the price was right. Having sold the trailer I now had space in my garage, so I laid down a carpet to exercise on and bought a treadmill for my walks to nowhere. I have time on my hands and an unfilled dance card so I'm sure I'll come up with a Plan B for what to do the rest of my life, perhaps I'll try writing. I wonder what the odds for success are for writers?

The Art Show Gypsy

www.ingramcontent.com/pod-product-compliance
Lightning Source LLC
Chambersburg PA
CBHW071814170526
45167CB00003B/1310